Fifty-Six Days

Ablaze

AN 8-WEEK TEEN DEVOTIONAL

Fifty-Six Days

Ablaze

AN 8-WEEK TEEN DEVOTIONAL

RON LUCE

CREATION
HOUSE
BOOKS ABOUT SPIRIT-LED LIVING
ORLANDO, FLORIDA

Creation House
Strang Communications Company
600 Rinehart Road
Lake Mary, FL 32746
Phone: (407) 333-3132
Fax: (407) 333-7100

Cover photo: Ron Luce and his wife, Katie, with participants in the Teen Mania
1994 summer missions program. Photo by Gary Chapman.

First printing, September 1994
Second printing, November 1994
Third printing, March 1995

Fifty-six Days Ablaze has been designed to help you become an incredible man or woman of God. You are not too young to start getting your roots down deep. It's great that you have made a commitment to God. Now it's time to seek Him with all your heart and get strong by learning His Word and applying it to your life.

There are so many airheaded Christians all over North America, and God is tired of it. We need to prove our seriousness with Him by getting up every morning to seek Him.

This discipleship manual has been designed for you to use at least fifteen minutes a day. I suggest you get up early, earlier than usual, to hear God's voice. He will help you understand what a *real* Christian is and how you can be an excited, committed Christian for the rest of your life.

For this manual to set your spirit ablaze with love for God, you need to commit to four specific things for the next eight weeks.

1. Get up fifteen minutes early every day and work your way through this book. Not every other day. Not skipping for a few days at a time. *Every single day for the next eight weeks.* This will produce serious growth in your Christian life. Are you ready to become strong?

2. Find an accountability partner – a radical friend of Christ who will stay in your face to make sure you do it every day. You and your partner should go through the manual together and talk to each other several times a week to find out how each of you is growing in the Lord.

3. Memorize Scripture verses every week. This may be a challenge at first, but with practice it will become easier. The benefit of having God's Word stored up in your heart is that it will be with you for the rest of your life.

4. Take notes at every church and youth service you attend and apply them to your life.

I am confident that if you do these things, pray and listen to the heart of God, your life will never be the same! You will be a world-changer for the rest of your life!

Consumed by the call,

Ron Luce
President, Teen Mania Ministries

COMMITMENT AGREEMENT

Fill out this commitment agreement and have it signed
before you begin this manual.

I, _____, commit to the four principles
for growth listed on page 5.

I will begin the discipleship manual on _____ (date)

and plan to finish by _____ (date).

_____   _____
your signature   date

_____   _____
signature of accountability partner   date

_____   _____
signature of youth pastor or parent   date

Table Of Contents

Week 1
What It Means to Live for Jesus   8

Week 2
Why Jesus Died   24

Week 3
What If I Don't Feel Anything?   40

Week 4
How to Grow in the Lord   56

Week 5
Why Music Matters   72

Week 6
What Is Real Worship?   88

Week 7
Friends for Life   104

Week 8
How to Pray   120

Week 1

WHAT IT MEANS TO LIVE FOR JESUS

Week 1 Memory Verses

MATTHEW 22:37-40
Jesus replied: "Love the Lord your God with all your heart, and with all your soul and with all your mind." This is the first and greatest commandment. And the second is like it: "Love your neighbor as yourself." All the Law and the Prophets hang on these two commandments.

JOHN 3:16
For God so loved the world that he gave his one and only Son, that whoever believes in him shall not perish but have eternal life.

1 JOHN 3:1
How great is the love the Father has lavished on us, that we should be called children of God! And that is what we are! The reason the world does not know us is that it did not know him.

1 JOHN 2:15-17
Do not love the world or anything in the world. If anyone loves the world, the love of the Father is not in him. For everything in the world — the cravings of sinful man, the lust of his eyes and the boasting of what he has and does — comes not from the Father but from the world. The world and its desires pass away, but the man who does the will of God lives forever.

JOHN 21:15
When they had finished eating, Jesus said to Simon Peter, "Simon son of John, do you truly love me more than these?"

JOHN 14:15
If you love me, you will obey what I command.

JOHN 15:13
Greater love has no one than this, that he lay down his life for his friends.

Week 1

WHAT IT MEANS TO LIVE FOR JESUS

DAY 1

Matthew 22:37-40

Jesus replied: "Love the Lord your God with all your heart and with all your soul and with all your mind." This is the first and greatest commandment. And the second is like it: "Love your neighbor as yourself." All the Law and the Prophets hang on these two commandments.

Take five minutes right now to memorize Matthew 22:37-40.

WHAT HAD PROMPTED JESUS TO GIVE THIS REPLY?

Hearing that Jesus had silenced the Sadducees, the Pharisees got together. One of them, an expert in the law, tested Him with this question, "Teacher, which is the greatest commandment in the Law?"

Jesus replied, " 'Love the Lord your God with all your heart and with all your soul and with all your mind.' This is the first and greatest commandment. And the second is like it, 'Love your neighbor as yourself.' All the Law and the prophets hang on these two commandments."

Great! You are saved. You have given your heart to Jesus. You have confessed Him as Lord. He is your boss! You no longer live for the world – you live for God.

Jesus tells us what that means in this passage. The most important thing you can do is live for God with your whole heart. We must love Him with all of our hearts because He is more important than anyone or anything else.

List some things in your life that you love with all of your heart and that you put a lot of energy into, such as football, cheerleading and music.

1.

2.

3.

What does it mean to you to love Jesus with all of your heart and mind?

List some other things that you think about a lot.

1.

2.

3.

How do you honor the Lord with all of the strength in your life?

When you think about being a Christian, you can get confused about what you are supposed to do and think and how you are supposed to act.

But *the most important* thing is loving Jesus with all your guts, all your soul, all your energy and strength, all your passion – basically with your *whole life*.

Does a boyfriend or girlfriend, money, movies, sports, music, clubs or activities have more priority than Jesus?

CHOOSE TO LOVE JESUS TODAY MORE THAN THESE THINGS THAT YOU HAVE LOVED IN THE PAST.

11

Week 1

WHAT IT MEANS TO LIVE FOR JESUS

DAY 2

John 3:16

> For God so loved the world that He gave His only begotten Son, that
> whoever believes in Him should not perish but have everlasting life
> (NKJV).

If you don't know this verse already, memorize it now.

The Bible says God loves us so much that He gave His only Son. When He saw
that the people on earth had a problem with sin infecting every part of their
lives and they needed some help desperately, He sent His Son.

He did not send an angel. He did not rain tracts from heaven to tell us how to
find Him. He sent Jesus, His Son. For God so loved the world that He gave His
very best.

The Bible says in 1 John 4:19 that we love Him because He loved us first. The
incredible gift that God gave when He gave Jesus is an awesome expression of
His love for us.

The only response we can have is to love Him back. That is what being a
Christian is all about – being in love with God and committing to love Him with
everything we have!

 **HOW DO YOU KNOW IF YOU LOVE GOD ENOUGH TO GIVE YOUR BEST?**

What are some other things that you have given your best to?

I want to challenge you to give your very best to God because He gave His very best for you.

Write down some ways you can show Him today that you want to give Him your best.

1.

2.

3.

4.

Meditate on John 3:16 all day today. Chew on it and think about what it means to give your *best* to God.

Do you still remember Matthew 22:37-40? Get it in your heart today.

TO BE A CHRISTIAN IS TO BE A LOYAL SUBJECT OF THE KING OF KINGS.

Week 1

WHAT IT MEANS TO LIVE FOR JESUS

DAY 3

1 John 3:1

> How great is the love the Father has lavished on us, that we should
> be called children of God! And that is what we are! The reason the
> world does not know us is that it did not know him.

Take five minutes right now to memorize this verse.

Please read the following before going on: Luke 7:36-50.

The focus of keeping your Christian life alive is to remember to love God with
your whole being.

We see in 1 John 3:1 that God has lavished His love on us. He even called us
His sons and daughters. The natural response when we receive so much love
from one person is to love him back.

I want you to think about it for just a second. God has called you His child. You
belong to Him. He has poured out His love for you. Just think about it. He did
not have to do it – He chose to.

We are able to see a great example of God's love in the story of the woman
who washed Jesus' feet with her tears. She was so incredibly grateful because
of how much she had been forgiven. She realized that Jesus loved her so much
that He did not condemn her or put her down. Instead He lifted her up.

Jesus' conclusion was:

He who is forgiven much loves much.

Take a moment to write in your own words what that means to you.

Think back for a moment on all the things you have thought or said or done that have broken the heart of God.

He has washed those all away. How much more grateful can we be? How much more in love can we be with God, who has forgiven us so much?

Our natural response, after having God's love blow our minds, is to pursue Him as fervently and aggressively as we possibly can – to live for Him and know Him better than we know anyone else in the world.

MAKE YOUR LIFE COUNT FOR ETERNITY – TODAY.

WHAT IT MEANS TO LIVE FOR JESUS

DAY 4

1 John 2:15-17

> Do not love the world or anything in the world. If anyone loves the world, the love of the Father is not in him. For everything in the world – the cravings of sinful man, the lust of his eyes and the boasting of what he has and does – comes not from the Father but from the world. The world and its desires pass away, but the man who does the will of God lives forever.

Take five minutes today to memorize and meditate on these verses.

Here the Bible tells us not to love the world or anything in the world.

Our lives are so caught up with this craze or that fad. We want this or we want that. We want to have what others say is fun. We want to be in this club or this sport. Most of the things end up placing us in sinful situations.

The Bible says not to love the world or what the world loves. Do not look with envy on the things the world covets.

List some things the world loves that you can see are clearly a ploy from the devil to distract people from God.

       1.

       2.

       3.

       4.

A lot of the music, movies, videos and other things the world loves are anti-God. They push us away from God. They drown out our love for God.

Some people decide to fall in love with God and follow Jesus, but they continue to love the things the world loves. Doing so drowns out their love for God.

Make a list here of some things you need to get out of your life to keep from drowning out your love for God.

       1.

       2.

       3.

       4.

Decide *now* to turn away from these things.

BE STRONG AND COURAGEOUS.

What It Means to Live for Jesus

Day 5

John 21:15

> When they had finished eating, Jesus said to Simon Peter, "Simon son of John, do you truly love me more than these?"

Take three minutes to memorize John 21:15.

Jesus was talking to Peter in this passage. After Jesus had risen from the dead, Peter was out fishing, and Jesus was on the shore. Peter ended up catching a big load and realized it was a miracle. He brought all the fish to shore and was sorting them when Jesus began to talk to him.

He asked, "Peter, do you love Me more than these?"

What was Jesus really talking about?

Obviously, Peter had been incredibly blessed by having this great fish load because it was going to produce a lot of money for him. He may have been thinking about how he could make some improvements on his house or buy a present for his wife or new clothes for himself.

Jesus was asking him a question He asks all of us:

Do you love Me more than these things I have blessed you with?

Do you love Me more than your clothes, your makeup and your popularity? Do you love Me more than your car, your stereo and the posters on your wall? Do you love Me more than your dreams or the things your parents or I have given you?

Do you love Jesus more than these things? In other words, are you willing to give them *all* up for Jesus? That poses the central question of whether or not we love Jesus with all that we have.

 ASK YOURSELF THIS QUESTION RIGHT NOW: DO YOU LOVE JESUS MORE THAN THE THINGS YOU HAVE IN YOUR ROOM AND ON YOUR WALLS?

If Jesus was in your bedroom right now asking you that question, what would He be referring to in your life?

Do you love Jesus more?

Think about how much you love the things in your room and the activities you are involved in.

How much time do you spend thinking about them?

How many hours do you play with them?

How excited are you to be involved with them?

Do you think about Jesus that much?

Are you that excited to be involved with Him?

Make a decision to reprioritize the things you love so that Jesus is number one in your life.

CHOOSE WHAT TO DIE FOR.

Week 1

WHAT IT MEANS TO LIVE FOR JESUS

DAY 6

John 14:15

If you love me, you will obey what I command.

Meditate on this verse all day!

What does it mean to love God? We have been talking all week about loving Him with everything we have.

Jesus says here if we are really going to love Him we must obey Him and submit to Him joyfully. We know that His desires are the best.

Many people think Jesus comes to spoil all our fun and to take away the zest in life.

That is wrong! Those are lies! He comes with life, life to the full (John 10:10).

If we are really going to love Him, we have to love and obey even if we do not understand why!

To love Him is to obey His commands.

List a few commands here that you have not obeyed as you should have recently.

1.

2.

3.

4.

Make a commitment today to submit to Him and then obey these things with all of your heart.

Have you met with your accountability partner this week?

WHAT IT MEANS TO LIVE FOR JESUS

DAY 7

John 15:13

> Greater love has no one than this, that one lay down his life for his friends.

Take five minutes to memorize this verse and think about it.

This is the true definition of love. We know Jesus loved us so much that He gave up His life for us. That is love.

I remember when my wife, Katie, and I had our first daughter, Hannah. She was just a small, helpless baby. How incredible was my love for her!

If for any reason her life had been in danger, in a second, without even thinking, I would have thrown my life out as a substitute for hers. It was a natural response. I would lay down my life for my daughter.

Jesus wants this same kind of commitment from us.

He wants us to love Him so much that we give up our lives, our plans, our careers, our pride and our selfishness to love Him.

Just imagine a guy in a war who is in a foxhole with a friend. In the middle of the war a grenade is thrown at them. They stare at each other, eye-to-eye. Without saying a word, one of the friends jumps on the grenade and is instantly blown to pieces.

The friend that is still alive sits there amazed that a man would give his life, his very life, so he could live. He goes over and picks up his friend's broken body and carries it back to camp. There he cries.

He realizes that this guy literally gave His life so that he could live. That is the kind of guy you could love because you know beyond a shadow of a doubt that he loved you first and gave you life.

That is the kind of person Jesus is.

We know He loves us because He gave His life for us. He is the kind of guy we can give our lives for – and not just our physical lives. We can give up the time we have here in the world so that everything – our goals, our desires, our careers – revolves around our love for Him.

What are some areas in your life that you need to give up?

How can you, in a practical way, lay down your life for Jesus today?

Let us remember that the thrust of our Christian lives is not what we do or how we look. The thrust is to love Jesus with everything we have and let the rest of our lives come from the love we have.

Take two or three minutes to review the verses you memorized this week.

MAKE SURE WHAT YOU ARE LIVING FOR IS WORTH DYING FOR.

Week 2

WHY JESUS DIED

Week 2 Memory Verses

ROMANS 6:23
For the wages of sin is death, but the gift of God is eternal life in Christ Jesus our Lord.

ROMANS 6:17
But thanks be to God that, though you used to be slaves to sin, you whole-heartedly obeyed the form of teaching to which you were entrusted.

JAMES 1:14-15
Each one is tempted when, by his own evil desire, he is dragged away and enticed. Then, after desire has conceived, it gives birth to sin; and sin, when it is full-grown, gives birth to death.

HEBREWS 9:22
In fact, the law requires that nearly everything be cleansed with blood, and without the shedding of blood there is no forgiveness.

ROMANS 6:10
The death he died, he died to sin once for all; but the life he lives, he lives to God.

JOHN 8:11
"No one, sir," she said. "Then neither do I condemn you," Jesus declared. "Go now and leave your life of sin."

HEBREWS 9:14
How much more, then, will the blood of Christ, who through the eternal Spirit offered himself unblemished to God, cleanse our consciences from acts that lead to death, so that we may serve the living God!

WHY JESUS DIED

DAY 1

Romans 6:23

> For the wages of sin is death, but the gift of God is eternal life in Christ Jesus our Lord.

Take a few minutes to memorize this verse right now.

Since we have established that being a real Christian is loving God with everything we have, this week we are going to look at exactly why Jesus died.

Sometimes the Christian message does not seem to make much sense. We do not understand why Jesus had to die.

Romans 3:23 says, "For all have sinned and fall short of the glory of God."

From these two verses we see there is a nature that is separating us from God. It is called *sin*. It is a nature that we are born with; we inherited it from Adam and Eve.

The Bible says in Genesis that God warned Adam not to touch the forbidden tree or he would surely die. The law of sin and death was implemented at that point.

Basically it said that if you sin you will die.

Now we know that Adam and Eve did not die physically as soon as they sinned. But they were separated from God. Instantly they died spiritually. They began to fill the world with people who were born spiritually dead. Ultimately, they died physically because the effect of sin is that you die.

The biggest problem is that when you are born, you are dead. Your body is alive, but you are dead spiritually. That means you are cut off from God.

Death is the natural result of going against God or being rebellious. Sin is going against God's commandments.

A lot of people look alive on the outside but are dead on the inside. This is because they are separated from God and are doing things God doesn't want them to do.

List some things you have done that may have been rebellious toward God.

1.

2.

3.

Many times we think we are having so much fun when we are sinning. Then afterward we feel really bad.

List some times you have felt empty, dry or dead after you rebelled against God.

1.

2.

3.

The question we need to ask is, Why did Jesus die? The answer is, Because there was a problem — sin. Sin had cut us off from God.

Get the verses from this past week into your heart and meditate on them all day!

WHY JESUS DIED

DAY 2

Romans 6:17

But thanks be to God that, though you used to be slaves to sin, you wholeheartedly obeyed the form of teaching to which you were entrusted.

Take five minutes to memorize this verse today.

The Bible says in Romans 6:17 that you used to be a slave to sin.

A slave is somebody who has no rights, who does what he is told, who does what he is supposed to do. He has no choice of his actions. Another power dictates everything he does.

That is exactly how it is before we are Christians. We are slaves to a sinful nature, a natural impulse to do things in rebellion toward God.

When we say that Jesus died to forgive our sins, that is true. But, even bigger than that, He died to help us get rid of our sinful nature.

We do things that are sins without even thinking about it. List some times this has happened in your own life.

1.

2.

3.

4.

When we say that Jesus has set us free, those are not little words.

Romans 6:18 says that we have been set free from sin and have become slaves to righteousness.

You have been set free from the sin nature that gripped you on the inside and forced you to be a slave.

This is good news!

Thank God today for forgiving you and setting you free!

Have you spent time with your accountability partner lately? If not, do it today.

WHY JESUS DIED

DAY 3

James 1:14-15

> Each one is tempted when, by his own evil desire, he is dragged away and enticed. Then, after desire has conceived, it gives birth to sin; and sin, when it is full-grown, gives birth to death.

Spend a few minutes now and memorize James 1:14-15.

James is talking about what happens when we sin.

First of all, God does not tempt us with sin. Sin comes when we get tempted by our own evil desire. Jesus said that from within the heart of man come evil desires, murders and envy.

So when the devil brings something along and we see it, the desire within our hearts causes us to want it, hate it or covet it. That is how we get enticed into sin.

After desire conceives, it gives birth to sin. God does not put sin in your life. It naturally happens when something comes across your path and you want it.

When sin is full-grown, it gives birth to death. You are dragged away from God.

List a few things that have enticed you in the past. You have wanted to do these things, but they are not right.

1.

2.

3.

4.

Now the exciting part comes when we realize that, through Christ, we are redeemed from even that desire to be enticed.

Jesus taught His disciples to pray: "Lead us not into temptation, but deliver us from the evil one" (Matthew 6:13). We can pray the same thing, and God will deliver us from temptation and from evil.

The good news is that we are no longer slaves to sin, but we are slaves to righteousness!

Take a moment right now and pray that God will deliver you from evil and enable you to walk in righteousness.

Spend three to four minutes now to review the verses for today and for the past week. Get them deep down in your soul!

WHY JESUS DIED

DAY 4

Hebrews 9:22

> In fact, the law requires that nearly everything be cleansed with blood, and without the shedding of blood there is no forgiveness.

Spend five minutes memorizing this verse.

The question we are answering this week is, Why did Jesus die?

Why did God's Son have to give His own life?

We have been talking about this "sin thing" the whole week. When we are talking about sin, we mean the conscious things we have done in disobedience to God's Word.

Look at Hebrews 9:22 again. The Bible says,

> In fact, the law requires that nearly everything be cleansed with blood, and without the shedding of blood there is no forgiveness.

Rebellion against God (which is sin) is so intense and incredibly serious that everyone deserves to die. That is what the law of sin and death is: If you sin, you die. If you go against God, you deserve eternal punishment.

God established the fact that if somebody sins, someone's blood has to be shed in order to get forgiveness. This blood represents the person's life!

In the Old Testament they sacrificed lambs. When they sacrificed a lamb, they asked God for forgiveness and watched the blood drain from the lamb. They realized that the sin should have cost them their lives, but instead the lamb was a substitute for them.

That is how incredibly serious their sin was to God. It cost somebody his life.

When Jesus came and died, He became the sacrificial lamb who took away the sins of the whole world. Because of the law of sin and death, somebody had to die to get rid of the sin.

Jesus was our substitute, our sacrifice. He gave His life so that we could have life. Because of this, we can give our lives for righteousness.

The world says that sin is just a mistake. People say, "I have a problem in my life." They do not like to identify it as sin.

God says sin is worthy of death, even the death of His own Son. That is how serious He is. He would not just forget it. The sin had to cost somebody His life.

Jesus chose to give up His life for us.

TAKE SOME TIME TO THANK JESUS FOR WHAT HE HAS DONE FOR YOU.

Week 2

WHY JESUS DIED

DAY 5

Romans 6:10

> The death he died, he died to sin once for all; but the life he lives, he lives to God.

Take two minutes to learn this verse.

 WHY DID JESUS DIE?

Jesus became the price that God paid in order to forgive our sins.

Let us say, for example, that you are going to buy a shirt. If you pay thirty dollars at the store, then the shirt is worth thirty dollars to you. If you lose the shirt, it is just as if you lost thirty dollars.

God had a price tag on us. That's because He had to buy us back when we became slaves. When somebody is made a slave, he cannot just get out of slavery for free. Somebody needs to pay for him to be set free.

So God had to decide what you're worth. Are you worth all the silver and gold on earth? Are you worth all the rubies and diamonds?

No, you are worth much more than that.

34

God said, "My Son, His blood – *that* is how much you are worth." He paid the highest price – His Son's blood. That is how much you are worth.

A little boy saved up his allowance and bought a toy boat kit and put it together. He dreamed about his boat at night and got up every day to play with it. It was his favorite toy.

One day he could not find the boat. He looked and looked, but he could not find it. He cried. He told his parents. He sulked. He was very sad. Nothing his parents did for him could bring him joy.

About a month later, the boy was walking past a shop in town. In the window stood his little boat – for sale. He ran into the shop. "Please, please – that is my boat," he said to the shopkeeper. "Give it to me."

"I am sorry," the shopkeeper replied. "I cannot give it to you. But I will sell it to you."

"But I already paid for it once," the boy explained.

The shopkeeper told him he had bought it from someone else. He said again to the little boy, "I cannot give it to you, but I will sell it to you."

"But I have already paid for it once," the little boy insisted.

Finally the little boy ran home to tell his parents. After hearing the whole story, his parents went to the shop and paid for the boat again.

That is the same way Jesus paid the price. He created us. But we were put into the slavery of sin, and there was a price to pay to redeem us from that slavery.

Thank Jesus for the price He paid just for you. He bought you back again!

CHRIST OVERCAME THE WORLD
SO IT WOULD NOT OVERCOME US.

WHY JESUS DIED

DAY 6

John 8:11

> "No one, sir," she said. "Then neither do I condemn you," Jesus declared. "Go now and leave your life of sin."

Take time this morning to memorize John 8:11.

We are talking about why Jesus had to die.

Ultimately, it was to buy us back from sin. He paid a price so that we could be forgiven of sin.

What does it mean to be forgiven?

Forgiveness means that I give up my right to strike back, even though I deserve that right.

God had every reason in the world to strike back at us, because in our rebellion we struck out at Him. But He chose to give up the right to punish us and send us to hell. Instead He forgave us. The only condition is that we have faith in His Son Jesus.

In John 8:3-11 we read the story of how several people had caught a woman in adultery and brought her to Jesus.

They said, "Jesus, Jesus, what do You think we should do? She should be stoned, don't You think?" They were all ready to condemn her.

Usually, when we see a problem in somebody else's life, we are ready to condemn him and put him down.

Jesus is not like that.

He said, "If any of you is without sin, throw the first stone."

He did not condemn her. Jesus does not condemn sinners. He forgives them and releases them from their captivity of slavery to sin.

We are forgiven just as He forgave the woman in verse 11. He does not condemn her either. He tells her to go and leave her life of sin.

List some habits or sinful things you have done that you know Jesus has released you from since you asked forgiveness.

1.

2.

3.

List some other habits in your life that are still tearing you down and that you need to be set free from.

1.

2.

3.

When we receive real forgiveness, it is just like the woman we read about last week. She kissed Jesus' feet because she was so grateful to be forgiven. She was so in love with Jesus because she had been released from such a heavy burden.

Take a moment to thank Jesus and worship Him for setting you free from such a big burden. Meet with your accountability partner and share with him or her what you have learned this week!

WHY JESUS DIED

DAY 7

Hebrews 9:14

> How much more, then, will the blood of Christ, who through the eternal Spirit offered himself unblemished to God, cleanse our consciences from acts that lead to death, so that we may serve the living God.

Spend five minutes today memorizing this verse.

When Jesus forgives us, He does not just sort of forgive. In fact, as we have learned this week, He takes away the very desire that we have to do evil things. He sets us free. He does a deep and thorough cleaning. The Bible says here in Hebrews that He even cleanses our consciences.

So many times after living a life of sin, our consciences become hardened, and we do not even care if we sin; we do not even realize it is wrong. We get hardened to God. After so many years of living in sin, it is possible to operate in a rebellious lifestyle without even feeling bad about it.

The Bible says that when Jesus forgives us, He actually cleanses our minds and our consciences so we become sensitive to God again. God is wanting to speak to us, but when our hearts and consciences get hardened with sin, we cannot hear Him — even if He were to speak with a megaphone.

List some areas where your conscience has been hardened or calloused so that it does not seem wrong anymore to do a particular sin.

1.

2.

3.

Hebrews 10:22 says,

> Having our hearts sprinkled to cleanse us from a guilty conscience and having our bodies washed with pure water.

Jesus has forgiven us for our past. He has forgiven our future. He has cleansed our minds, our hearts and our consciences so that we can live in absolute purity. This is why Jesus died.

He died to make you a brand-new person. As He forgives you, His Spirit comes to live in you. He thoroughly cleanses you and makes you sensitive to God so that you can have an incredible personal relationship with Him and hear the Father speak to you.

Review this verse and the commitments you have made this entire week. Worship and thank God for redeeming you and setting you free from your past, your present and your future. Thank Him for giving you a clean conscience and for delivering you from the sin nature, the nature that leads ultimately to death.

WHAT GOD HAS FORGIVEN WE CAN ALSO FORGET.

The reason Jesus died for you is the same reason He died for every person on earth. Think and pray about how you can tell people what Jesus did. Have you ever thought about going overseas on a missions trip? Look in the back of this book for information on how you could do it.

eek 3

WHAT IF I DON'T FEEL ANYTHING?

WEEK 3 MEMORY VERSES

MATTHEW 7:24
Therefore everyone who hears these words of mine and puts them into practice is like a wise man who built his house on the rock.

ROMANS 10:9-10
That if you confess with your mouth, "Jesus is Lord," and believe in your heart that God raised him from the dead, you will be saved. For it is with your heart that you believe and are justified, and it is with your mouth that you confess and are saved.

JAMES 4:8
Come near to God and he will come near to you.

PHILIPPIANS 4:8
Whatever is true, whatever is noble, whatever is right, whatever is pure, whatever is lovely, whatever is admirable – if anything is excellent or praiseworthy – think about such things.

2 CORINTHIANS 5:7
We live by faith, not by sight.

Week 3

WHAT IF I DON'T FEEL ANYTHING?

DAY 1

Matthew 7:24

> Therefore everyone who hears these words of mine and puts them into practice is like a wise man who built his house on the rock.

Take a couple of minutes to memorize this verse.

Some people, when they give their lives to the Lord, have a dramatic experience. Some weep, laugh, get excited or are amazed at what God has done for them. Some people do not feel much change at all.

This week we are going to talk about how to build your house on Jesus, *not* on feelings!

Matthew 7:24 talks about the wise man who builds his house on the rock. This parable helps you understand how to build your life on Jesus. When you become a Christian, you do not leave Jesus at the door of your life and continue with your daily activities as before.

Jesus says that to live for Him you need to build your life on Him, the Rock, and establish every part of your life in a solid way on Him. You may have felt incredible warm fuzzies when you first gave your life to Jesus. Or you may have felt nothing at all. You may have been wondering why some people feel something and others do not.

The answer is, nobody knows why. God just deals with different people in different ways.

A good example here is the story of the woman who wept when she was forgiven for so much (Luke 7:36-50). She was emotionally stirred at the discovery of how much she had been forgiven. She may not have been as emotional the next few weeks, but still she had been forgiven.

Maybe you felt excited and had a lot of gushy feelings when you first gave your life to Jesus, but now you do not feel anything. Warm fuzzies may come and go, but we must develop a steadfast life in Jesus.

List some things you can do to help you build your life on Jesus.

1.

2.

3.

4.

What do you think it means to build your life on the Rock of Jesus?

Do it today!

IT IS NOT IMPORTANT WHAT YOU FEEL. JUST KEEP BUILDING YOUR LIFE ON JESUS – NO MATTER WHAT!

WHAT IF I DON'T FEEL ANYTHING?

DAY 2

Romans 10:9-10

> If you confess with your mouth, "Jesus is Lord," and believe in your heart that God raised him from the dead, you will be saved. For it is with your heart that you believe and are justified and it is with your mouth that you confess and are saved.

Take five minutes today to get this verse into your heart.

We need to guide our lives by what God's Word says, not by our feelings. Sometimes when we feel really excited about a thing, we are, of course, more prone to do it. If we do not have those feelings, we probably will not want to do that thing.

So many Christians go up and down because they guide their lives by their feelings and not by the Word of God. When some people go forward at an altar call, they feel very enthusiastic and excited. But when they leave and have their own quiet times of reading the Bible and talking to God, they do not feel any warm fuzzies, and so they do not want to keep up with their quiet times. We have to build our lives on the stability of God's Word.

The Bible says in Romans 10:9-10 that if you confess Jesus as your Lord and believe in your heart that He was raised from the dead, you are saved.

You are saved not just because you feel saved. Sometimes you do not feel saved at all. But you have to go back to the Word.

 **ASK YOURSELF, HAVE I CONFESSED JESUS AS MY LORD? WHAT DOES THAT MEAN TO YOU?**

It means He is your boss, your chief. You have submitted to Him.

Have you said, "Lord Jesus, You are my Lord, and I believe in my heart that You have been raised from the dead"?

Then you are saved!

It does not matter whether you feel like it or not. If the Word of God says it is true, it is true. It does not matter what feelings the devil may bring my way. I have to build my life and faith on God's Word.

God said that if I confess Jesus as Lord and believe He was raised from the dead, I am saved.

Boom! I am saved! No question about it.

You have to have an incredible confidence about what God says. What He says is true no matter what you feel.

This is the fundamental building block of your life in Christ. You build it on His Word. You believe it because God said it, no matter what you feel.

Circumstances and people will come into your life and make your feelings change. But that does not mean that what God has done in your life has changed.

Don't worry about having the feelings. Just concentrate on having a pure heart and living for Him and letting God clean up your life.

Keep meditating on and memorizing the Word of God!

Have you checked with your accountability partner today?

Week 3

WHAT IF I DON'T FEEL ANYTHING?

DAY 3

James 4:8

Come near to God and he will come near to you.

Take three minutes to memorize and meditate on this verse.

So what if you do not feel anything? What should you do?

You need to live a life of obedience because you love Jesus – whether you feel anything or not.

It is just like when you are married. Sometimes you feel in love, and sometimes you do not feel in love. The fact is that if you have made a decision to love, then you do love the person. You need to do things that will draw your hearts closer and closer together.

James 4:8 says that if we come near to God, He will come near to us. What does that really mean?

If you do things to focus on God, to draw close to Him, then He will draw close to you. The closer you get to Him, the more you feel Him near. But you do not have to feel Him to know He is near. God said that He will never leave you or forsake you (Hebrews 13:5). He will not leave you, whether you feel as if He is there or not.

List some things you could do to draw closer to God today.

1.

2.

3.

4.

 Once you do these things, what will you do if you do not feel anything?

If you keep quoting the Word and are committed to what you know is true, it does not matter what you feel. The Word says it is true, no matter how you feel.

Your feelings will eventually follow. Do not give up. Keep pressing in to Christ, and you *will* feel Him near.

Meditate on James 4:8 all day long and really believe it!

Disappointment is not defeat unless you stop trying.

Week 3

WHAT IF I DON'T FEEL ANYTHING?

DAY 4

Read: Acts 16:16-40

We can learn a lot from the story of Paul and Silas in jail.

Paul and Silas worshipped God in the midst of the chains that bound them in prison. As they worshipped Him, the awesome presence of the living God came in. The place was shaken, the doors flew open, and the chains fell off.

As you get into the awesome presence of the incredible, sovereign, living, holy God, He can stir up your emotions (the way you feel, what you sense physically).

You may wonder how you can feel the same awesome presence of an incredible God early in the morning when you are barely awake.

 WHAT DOES IT TAKE TO GET INTO THE PRESENCE OF GOD?

When you find yourself in tough situations and do not feel God's presence, concentrate on loving Him more and worshipping Him as Paul and Silas did.

Then you realize God is there all the time, whether you feel Him or not.

When you really worship Him, you will feel His presence. When the presence of the living God comes, and you are completely focused on worshipping, you cannot help but experience His closeness.

 ARE YOU IN A TOUGH SITUATION?

ARE YOU HAVING A HARD TIME FEELING THE PRESENCE OF GOD?

If your answer is yes to either of these questions, then worship Him *today!*

Do not wait until tomorrow.

Worship Him today, and His presence will come in!

Take eight minutes today and review all the memory verses you have learned.

Week 3

WHAT IF I DON'T FEEL ANYTHING?

DAY 5

Philippians 4:8

> Whatever is true, whatever is noble, whatever is right, whatever is pure, whatever is lovely, whatever is admirable – if anything is excellent or praiseworthy – think about such things.

Take five minutes today to memorize this verse.

The Bible says we have to build our lives on the Word of God, not on what we feel. Building our lives on His Word has to do with memorizing it, chewing on it, listening to it and chewing on it some more.

If you are going to build your life on the Word of God, then you have to meditate on things like this:

> God has taken your sins away from you as far as the east is from the west (Psalm 103:12).

> Your life is hidden with God in Christ (Colossians 3:3).

> You are seated with Christ in heavenly places (Ephesians 2:6).

> You have been redeemed by the blood of the Lamb (1 Corinthians 6:20).

You need to meditate on this and realize it is true. No matter whether you feel it or not, it is true because God's Word says it.

You build your life by meditating on the truth.

The Bible promises, in Philippians 4:9, that if you do this, the God of peace will be with you.

Let your mind be set on the truth of God's promises today!

HAPPINESS COMES IN STRIVING FOR HOLINESS.

WHAT IF I DON'T FEEL ANYTHING?

DAY 6

2 Corinthians 5:7

We live by faith, not by sight.

Spend three minutes meditating on this verse. What does it mean to you?

When I first committed my life to the Lord, I felt extremely excited. But there have definitely been times since then when I have not felt much at all.

I have had to continue to read the Scripture, get up every morning, keep serving Him and keep loving Him even when I do not feel really excited.

According to 2 Corinthians 5:7, we cannot live by what we see. We live by our faith and confidence in knowing that God's Word is right no matter what we think or feel.

Walk by faith, not by what you see.

When it looks as if God has abandoned you or everyone has turned against you, it does not matter because you have faith that is bigger than sight. Faith is more important than sight, and you are believing God.

List some situations or circumstances you have experienced where it seemed as if God was not with you.

1.

2.

3.

4.

Think about the faith you have in the living God and how His Word will carry you through the tough circumstances.

Think about some Scripture verses that apply to the circumstances you just listed.

All day today I want you to think about this verse. Chew on it all day long: I live by faith, not by sight. I live by faith in the awesome, holy, living, incredible God, and not by sight or feelings.

Set some goals today about basing your life on the Word of God. For example, I will have faith for my brother's salvation even though he refuses to go to church with me.

Be sure to meet with your accountability partner this week.

What If I Don't Feel Anything?

Day 7

You have to be *committed* as a Christian to loving God and living for Him even when do not feel anything.

In fact, it would be a good thing for you to make a commitment to remain a Christian whether or not you have another "fuzzy feeling" the rest of your life.

Live by faith with your confidence in the Word of God.

You must love Him and serve Him even if all others turn their backs and you never get excited about another thing in your whole life.

Build your life on the Rock of Jesus Christ and on the confidence that His Word is true no matter how you feel.

Would You Take a Moment Now and Make a Commitment to God?

Tell Him: Lord, no matter how I feel, whether I am excited or not, I am going to commit to build my life step by step, day by day, on Your Word.

Now that you have said it, do it!

Review the verses you have learned so far. Do you still remember them? Get them in your heart today.

What are you doing with your life to glorify Jesus? Make a list of some ways you could bring glory to Him in your own unique way or through your own personal life circumstances:

1.

2.

3.

Make a commitment to try these things during the following week.

I AM IN THIS THING BECAUSE IT IS TRUE AND BECAUSE IT IS RIGHT — NO MATTER WHAT ANYONE SAYS ABOUT ME.

Week 4

HOW TO GROW IN THE LORD

WEEK 4 MEMORY VERSES

HEBREWS 6:1
Therefore let us leave the elementary teachings about Christ and go on to maturity.

MATTHEW 5:6
Blessed are those who hunger and thirst for righteousness, for they will be filled.

ROMANS 12:2
Do not conform any longer to the pattern of this world, but be transformed by the renewing of your mind.

1 PETER 2:2-3
Like newborn babies, crave pure spiritual milk, so that by it you may grow up in your salvation, now that you have tasted that the Lord is good.

1 CORINTHIANS 3:1-3
Brothers, I could not address you as spiritual but as worldly—mere infants in Christ. I gave you milk, not solid food, for you were not yet ready for it. Indeed, you are still not ready. You are still worldly. For since there is jealousy and quarreling among you, are you not worldly? Are you not acting like mere men?

JOHN 14:15
If you love me, you will obey what I command.

Week 4

HOW TO GROW IN THE LORD

DAY 1

Hebrews 6:1

> Therefore let us leave the elementary teachings about Christ and go on to maturity.

Take three minutes to meditate on this verse and memorize it. What does it mean to you?

Read Hebrews 5:11 - 6:3.

When you become a Christian, it is like becoming a baby all over again. Spiritually, it is just as if you were an infant. But it is important for you to grow.

How do you grow in the Lord? How do you get strong in the Lord?

According to Hebrews 5:11 - 6:3, as a baby you live on milk. If you are serious about your walk with God, start drinking the milk of God's Word. You need to get your nutrition from God's Word. But if you drink milk your whole life, you will not get the nutrition you need to continue growing.

A lot of people have been in church for a very long time and are still babies in Christ. These verses are admonishing those people who have not grown beyond infancy. They are unable to understand the deep things of God. They are not hungry or thirsty for the deep things of God. They are just there.

How do you feed yourself?

You read the Word and chew on it until it gets down in your heart and spirit. You meditate on it, and it helps you grow up and understand things. It also gives you wisdom beyond your years.

We need to get nutrition from the milk of the Word so we can get to the meat of the Word and feast on the deep things of God.

So many times you hear only teachings about the same old things your whole life. God wants us to grow up so we are not just being taught about the simple things such as:

Not cussing

Not listening to ungodly music

Not having ungodly friends

Not engaging in sex before you are married

You have heard these things for so long. Now is the time to mature and grow strong so you can learn the deep riches of who God is.

 ASK YOURSELF:

In the next month how much do you want to grow in the Lord?

In six months how much stronger do you want to be in the Lord?

In a year how much fruit of the Spirit do you want to have in your life?

How much more do you want to look like Jesus?

PRAY THAT GOD WILL GIVE YOU A PASSION TO GROW IN HIM. AND EXPECT HIM TO DO IT!

Week 4

HOW TO GROW IN THE LORD

DAY 2

Matthew 5:6

Blessed are those who hunger and thirst for righteousness, for they will be filled.

Take three minutes to memorize and meditate on this verse. What does it mean to you?

 ARE YOU HUNGRY AND THIRSTY FOR RIGHTEOUSNESS IN EVERY AREA OF YOUR LIFE?

Righteousness means that you are not embarrassed about any part of your life in front of God. It means that He is pleased with all areas of your life. You are in right standing with God.

To understand God and who He is, you need to hunger and thirst for the milk and the meat of the Word. If you are going to grow, you must long for it.

It is important, first of all, to be in love with God. It is important to understand why Jesus died. It is important to know that we live by faith and not by sight.

Keep your passion and grow in God as you have never grown before. Feast on Him, and eat the milk and the meat of His Word even when you do not feel like it.

When you were young, your mom made you eat spinach even when you didn't like it. You told her you didn't like it, but she said to go ahead and eat it. If you wanted to be like Popeye, she said, you would have to eat it.

You were forced to eat things and take vitamins that you did not really want. You'd rather have eaten junk food, but you had to eat good food that would help you grow stronger.

It is the same with the Word of God. You may hunger and thirst after things that do not help you grow. But it is time to change – to hunger and thirst after the Word of God so you will grow.

At times you may even need to force yourself to memorize and meditate on the Word. Only by doing so will you get stronger and stronger.

Meditate today on Matthew 5:6.

Week 4

HOW TO GROW IN THE LORD

DAY 3

Romans 12:2

Do not conform any longer to the pattern of this world, but be transformed by the renewing of your mind.

Take five minutes right now to memorize this verse.

I often say, "Lord, I want to change. I want to grow in You. I don't want to have the same problems." But how, in a very practical sense, have our lives changed?

The Bible says you have to be transformed, or changed, by renewing your mind or changing the way you think.

You must first change your mind. Once you change your mind, the way you think will change; then what you say will change and what you do will change. Many times we want to change what we do or say, but the way we think remains the same.

The Bible says here that the only way to change is by renewing your mind. In other words, you have to change the way you think because you have been brainwashed by the world to think the way the world thinks.

Now that you are a Christian, start thinking the way God thinks.

The best way to renew your mind is to memorize Scripture and meditate on it. Meditating on Scripture means to chew on it all day. Meditate on your Scripture memory verses every day. Keep chewing on the Word until it becomes such a part of you that you think that way naturally.

The more verses you plug into your mind, the more your mind and your life will change. Then you will act differently and treat people differently.

Begin to chew on the verse you memorized today.

MAKE A DETERMINATION OUT LOUD:
"I AM GOING TO BE CHANGED BY RENEWING MY MIND."

Make a list of some things you think about but should not. Find some Scripture verses that deal with these things and memorize them.

1.

Verse:

2.

Verse:

3.

Verse:

4.

Verse:

Every time you think about those things, pull out your Scripture verse and think about what the Word of God says.

Try it today and see for yourself how it works!

Have you met with your accountability partner this week? Ask him or her to hold you accountable to grow in the Lord.

Week 4

HOW TO GROW IN THE LORD

DAY 4

1 Peter 2:2-3

> Like newborn babies, crave pure spiritual milk, so that by it you may grow up in your salvation, now that you have tasted that the Lord is good.

Take four minutes and memorize this verse today.

We have been talking about being hungry for God. Think about what it means to crave, desire and have a passion for the Word of God, to yearn for the pure spiritual milk, the Word of God that will feed your soul and help you grow up.

The Scripture admonishes us here to "grow up" in our salvation. It is time for us to grow up.

Look in the mirror this morning and say to yourself: "Grow up in your salvation. Don't be a lame, yellow-bellied, chicken-livered baby your whole life."

Look at yourself and say, "I have to grow up today. I cannot be a baby today. I have to get into the Word of God."

How do you grow up? By thirsting for pure spiritual milk and renewing your mind in the Word of God today.

It is a matter of admonishing and exhorting yourself to grow up and quit being a baby. Nobody else can make you grow up. Nobody else can make you eat.

You can lead a horse to water, but you cannot make him drink it.

You can have the Word of God all around you, but no one can force you to meditate on it. No one can force you to put it into your mind.

You must decide to grow up in Jesus' name. You must decide that you are not going to be a thumb-sucking little baby your whole life.

DETERMINE ALOUD: "I AM GOING TO CRAVE PURE SPIRITUAL MILK AND GROW UP TODAY."

Pray that today, and review your memory verses to increase your spiritual strength.

Week 4

HOW TO GROW IN THE LORD

DAY 5

1 Corinthians 3:1-3

> Brothers, I could not address you as spiritual but as worldly – mere infants in Christ. I gave you milk, not solid food, for you were not yet ready for it. Indeed, you are still not ready for it. You are still worldly. For since there is jealousy and quarreling among you, are you not worldly? Are you not acting like mere men?

Spend some time reading these verses over and over until you memorize them.

In this verse Paul is rebuking the Christians. He says, "I have been wanting to treat you guys like you are grown up, but you are still babies!"

As I travel to youth conventions in America, I see many young people come to the altar time and time again. They are not becoming men and women. They are still babies in the Lord.

Sometimes I feel like saying the same thing Paul said here: You are mere infants! I wanted to talk to you about the deep things of God and the deep mysteries of the Scripture that would really blow your mind, but you people are still worldly and dealing with worldly issues. I wanted to give you something that you could sink your teeth into, but you are still playing around with the elementary things. You still have jealousy and quarreling among you.

 ARE YOU STILL WORLDLY IN SOME AREAS?

Think about your own life this morning as you are reading this. Are you still preoccupied with the world? Are you backbiting — talking about other people? Are you still doing things that are juvenile and elementary?

God wants you to grow up! He wants to do things for you, but you have to stop doing things that only babies in Christ do and start doing some things that will put the Word of God in your life and help you to grow up.

Look in the mirror this morning and exhort yourself to stop acting like a baby.

Make a list of worldly things you have done over the last couple of weeks.

1.

2.

3.

4.

Ask God to forgive you for those things. Decide to be strong in Him in these areas.

Pray that God will help you get over these things by the authority and power of the Spirit.

Ask Him to make you a strong man or woman of God today.

Tell Him you do not want to be a baby your whole life, but you want to grow up in the deep things of God.

WE CANNOT BE HAPPY IF WHAT WE BELIEVE IS DIFFERENT FROM WHAT WE DO!

HOW TO GROW IN THE LORD

DAY 6

John 14:15

If you love me, you will obey what I command.

After you learn John 14:15, review 1 Corinthians 3:1-3.

Let us talk today for a few minutes about solid food.

In 1 Corinthians Paul wrote that he wanted to give the Corinthians solid food, but they were not ready for it. God wants to make us into solid Christians, building our lives on His Word.

As you were growing up physically, you needed more than milk. You might have started eating mashed up vegetables, then whole vegetables and later some little pieces of meat. As your teeth came in, you ate bigger chunks of food.

It is the same way in Christ. As soon as you learn the elementary principles, God deals with you in other areas. He may give you mashed up vegetables, then whole vegetables, then big chunks of meat.

Paul said God had shown him many awesome things that he could not even write about because the people could not comprehend them.

Your pastor or youth pastor may talk to you about some really awesome things, but what they say goes right over your head because you are still a baby in

Christ. They could be talking about the deep riches of God that you have never heard before, and it is blowing right by you.

Why?

Because you are still at such an elementary stage that you are not ready for the deep things.

These deep things I am talking about include:

God's glimpse of your future

What you are going to do with your life

How He wants to use you to change the world

How He wants to use you to change the people in your school

Maybe the kid who sits next to you in geometry is going through some incredibly tough times. God may want you to share some of His words with him – words that would blow his mind and make him fall on his face.

GOD WANTS TO TEACH YOU DEEP THINGS ABOUT WHO HE IS SO YOU CAN EXPERIENCE HOW AWESOME HE IS.

He wants you to get so blown away by His presence, as Moses did, that your face glows and people look at you and say, "Man, where have you been?" Then you can turn around and say that you have been in the presence of God.

He wants to share many incredible things with you, but only if you tell yourself: "Quit being a baby. I am going to grow up. I want solid food today. I am going to meditate on God's Word."

Meditate on some of the Scripture verses we have discussed this week, and start chewing on some solid food today.

Are you getting in your partner's face? Challenge each other to meditate on the Word more and get into the deep things of God!

 Week 4

How to Grow in the Lord

Day 7

We have talked about how to grow. We have talked about how to be in love with God and hunger and thirst for the Word of God.

It is time to make a decision!

You cannot go through life hoping that you stay strong and do not fall away from God. If you say, "I hope I am going to grow up in the Lord; I hope I am going to get my roots deep in God," then you are not going to make it.

At a recent youth convention, a man came to the altar to commit his life to the Lord. "Boy, I hope I make it," he said.

"With that attitude you will not make it," I told him. "You are telling me it is not your responsibility whether you do it or not. You just hope God will help you."

God will help you. That is not the question.

You have to make a decision that, come hell or high water, you are not turning back. Dig into the deep things of God and transform your life by renewing your mind and chewing on the Word.

You cannot just hope to do it.

I was already in college studying to be a preacher when I decided to have quiet times first thing in the morning. We think we will be less busy tomorrow or next week, but it won't happen. I was busy with studies, friends, having fun and exercising. But no matter how tired or busy I was, it had to be a priority for me to get into the Word of God and learn all the things I needed to know to live an awesome life in Christ.

I set my alarm clock, and the next morning I was going to get up and do it. The alarm went off. My head was smashed on the pillow, and I did not want to get up. I finally forced myself to get up and splash cold water on my face, look in the mirror and say, "Get hungry. Wake up!" I opened up the door and let the cold winter air blow in. I got out my Bible and began to read and study it.

The next day I did the same thing. Eventually I had to get up earlier because I wanted *more* time to pray and read. Each day I sought God with all my heart.

I got closer to God than I had ever been before. I made better grades and learned more. I exercised more. I earned more money at the jobs I had.

God blesses you when you make Him a priority. It does not matter if you are thirteen or nineteen or fifteen. You need to make a decision now to hunger for God. Transform your life by renewing your mind. Build your house on the Rock.

 WILL YOU MAKE THAT DECISION?

Say this: "In Jesus' name I am going to be a steadfast man or woman of God who will not play games or go up and down. I will grow, not because I feel like it, but because it's a matter of survival!"

Get the verses from the past four weeks into your heart. Take a step in your life, and grow in Christ.

WHY MUSIC MATTERS

Week 5 Memory Verses

EXODUS 23:2
Do not follow the crowd in doing wrong.

EPHESIANS 5:19-20
Speak to one another with psalms, hymns and spiritual songs. Sing and make music in your heart to the Lord, always giving thanks to God the Father for everything.

1 CORINTHIANS 10:31
Whether you eat or drink or whatever you do, do it all for the glory of God.

Week 5

WHY MUSIC MATTERS

DAY 1

If Jesus has changed your heart, then His ways, His thoughts and His ideas should affect every area of your life, including music.

 **WHY WAS MUSIC CREATED?**

Judges 5:3 says, "I will make music to the Lord."

The Bible talks about angels making music to the Lord in heaven, blowing their trumpets and playing their harps. Music was created to glorify God. It was created as a way of expressing His awesomeness.

Today we have music that is played by every type of culture and religion.

There is nothing wrong with music. It was created to glorify God. The problem is with the people who express themselves in the music. What are they expressing?

Some people say a certain style of music is wrong, such as rock 'n' roll or heavy metal. Style is not the issue. The content and spirit behind the music are the issues.

Musicians write songs based on their experiences, good and bad. Some write about alcohol, drugs, immorality or other influences. They may be trying to prove a point or simply expressing their thoughts or feelings.

Some musicians choose to use the gifts that God has given them for themselves or for the world. Actually they are using their gifts for the devil. If these musicians are not Christians, they are using ideas that are not from the Lord. If their ideas are not from the Lord, there is only one other source for them.

It is scary when a person ignores the warnings and says, "I am going to listen to this music – period."

 WHY DOES MUSIC MATTER?

What is most important is not the style but the *spirit* of the person who is writing the music.

As you listen to music, it is influencing your mind. It enters your ears and mind, and you begin to think about the words. What if the person behind the music is a slave to sin, rebellious against God and totally controlled by their old nature?

Remember, you are transformed by the renewing of your mind. If your mind has been renewed by the Scripture and you go back to listening to that music, it tears down the Word of God that was planted in your mind.

You want to think God's thoughts, not what anybody else is thinking. If you listen to their music, then their thoughts, ideas and priorities will affect you – even though you don't want them to.

As an experiment today, pay careful attention to any music that you hear. Then ask yourself these questions:

Who wrote that?

What was in that person's heart?

What was in that person's mind?

What kind of experience did it come from?

What is that person trying to communicate?

Begin thinking differently about music.

Week 5

WHY MUSIC MATTERS

DAY 2

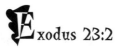xodus 23:2

Do not follow the crowd in doing wrong.

We are talking about what music you listen to. Music, especially in America and Europe, has become a subculture.

A certain kind of teenager in any high school in America can listen to a certain kind of music, whether it is pop, heavy metal, rap or some other style. That teenager may know all the groups playing that style and all the things they sing about. He may have all the latest CDs and videos by those groups. He may even begin to dress and dance like the people on the videos.

When a group within a culture acts and speaks in a distinct way, that group becomes a subculture — sort of a small group within a group.

You may not even realize that you wear black all the time or that you wear your hair a certain way. You may not notice that you have a certain type of attitude and say the same words used by the musicians you listen to.

A SUBCULTURE SUCKS YOU IN, AND YOU DON'T EVEN REALIZE IT.

You are being trained to think the way they think, to sing the way they sing, to look the way they look and to act the way they act.

The Bible speaks very clearly about this in Exodus 23:2. Do not give in to peer pressure. Do not do what the world wants you to do just because the world wants you to do it.

Just because these guys are famous rappers or rock stars does not mean that what they say to do is right. It doesn't mean that the way they say to dress is right.

You let these groups, or your peers, tell you what to think. You let them tell you what's cool and what's not cool. You have to be strong and realize that their philosophies and their lifestyles are affecting the way you think and the way you live. They're ripping you off, and you don't even realize it.

Compare the words of their music with the Word of God. If their words agree with God's Word, then listen to their music. If not, don't listen to it because you're going to get tricked. As a result, your foundation in Christ will not be stable.

IF YOU LIVE ON THE EDGE OF SIN, IT IS EASIER TO FALL.

Week 5

WHY MUSIC MATTERS

Day 3

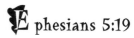

Ephesians 5:19

> Speak to one another with psalms, hymns and spiritual songs.

Take two minutes to memorize this verse. What exactly does this mean to you?

When we talk about the music we should listen to, does this mean we should only listen to church songs or hymns? Or should we sing very spiritual songs instead of listening to rock 'n' roll?

No, that is not what it means!

Music is an expression of your heart, an expression of an idea. It's an expression of something you are thinking about or something going on inside you. These are the things that inspire people when they write songs.

When it comes to music, you have to start asking yourself, Is the music I am listening to actually glorifying God? Is it lifting Him up?

You might think it's just mediocre music — not really of the devil, just mediocre. But is mediocre good enough?

Do you want to be a mediocre Christian?

Do you want to have a mediocre walk with God?

Do you want to make it into heaven as a mediocre person?

The Bible says that if you are going to sing a song, then let it be a spiritual song.

Let the song talk about how awesome God is, how cool He is, how great He is. Instead of wasting your energy glorifying your ideas, your experiences or your way of life, sing songs that lift up the King of kings and the Lord of lords.

Write Ephesians 5:19 in your own words.

How can you apply this practically to your life today?

WHY MUSIC MATTERS

DAY 4

Review Philippians 4:8.

It is interesting to me that a person can begin to meditate on the Word of God – to read it, learn it and memorize it – and then put on the headphones and listen to secular music that robs them of their peace and joy. Afterward, that person has lost his confidence in God and even believes he is backsliding.

In this verse, the Bible admonishes us to think only on what is holy, awesome and worthy of praise. With our minds set on these things, our mouths will lift up and glorify God.

> When I was a teenager, I was a "rock 'n' roller." After I was turned on to the Lord, I still liked my rock music. I listened to a little bit of Christian music, but I liked the other stuff. I didn't think the words really affected me.
>
> One day as I was driving in my car with the music on, I found myself singing the words to the song. Though I was a young Christian, I wondered why I was letting those words come out of my mouth.
>
> I thought, These words are not lifting God up. These are stupid words. I made a decision then that I was going to shut off the secular music and turn on the godly music.

Challenge yourself today to shut off anything that is not lifting Jesus up.

Do not let it go into your mind or come out of your mouth if it is not lifting up Jesus. I had to ask myself, If it is not affecting me, then why do I find myself singing it?

Music wraps up someone's values in a palatable package so that other people will like them. Music makes you want to listen to what they're singing about.

It's like a wolf in sheep's clothing. It seems friendly, but it's still a wolf planting ideas in your mind. You have to be smart enough to see through the lies. You have the responsibility to put godly things into your mind.

Shut some music off today!

YOU WILL NEVER ATTAIN SOMETHING YOU'VE NEVER HAD UNTIL YOU DO SOMETHING YOU'VE NEVER DONE.

Week 5

WHY MUSIC MATTERS

DAY 5

1 Corinthians 10:31

So whether you eat or drink or whatever you do, do it all for the glory of God.

As a result of the music you listen to, different things will come into your life. Music has a big effect on what you do. Think about how music makes you act.

WHAT ABOUT YOUR WALKMAN?

Maybe you're listening to your Walkman at school while you're sitting next to people you should be talking to. Maybe you're being distracted from opportunities to develop meaningful relationships with people at school – or at home – who could help you grow stronger in the Lord.

Think about it: You're listening to music because that subculture has sucked you in. Maybe you need to make a decision to put down the Walkman for a week, or only listen to it for an hour a day.

Some people are so addicted to music that they don't know what to do when they're not listening to something. Shut off the music, think about God and get into the Word. Have some quiet time with God.

WHAT ABOUT YOUR ROOM?

The music you listen to has an effect on the decor of your bedroom. Maybe you need to take a look at some of that and decide whether that poster is glorifying God – or is it just a heathen rock group or a stupid picture of girls or guys? If it's not glorifying God, it's just worldliness. Tear down the posters. Rearrange your room so it's clean and godly. Make it cool, but "godly" cool, not "worldly" cool.

WHAT ABOUT DANCING?

Many young people go to dances. I went to dances all the time. After I became a Christian I began to ask myself why. Here I was at a dance, moving my body and expressing myself to music that didn't glorify God. The whole thing was not glorifying God at all. I was just trying to pick up some girl. I decided that I would quit dancing.

You may think I'm taking this too far. But being a radical Christian means going "too far" in the right direction so you no longer get caught up in the wrong direction.

List some things involving music that you need to give up to do more to glorify God.

1.

2.

3.

Now list some fun things you can do that would glorify God.

1.

2.

3.

Get with your accountability partner and decide together to live sanctified lives.

GOD IS NOT TRYING TO STEAL YOUR FUN.
HE IS TRYING TO MAKE YOU INTO A WORLD-CHANGER!

Week 5

WHY MUSIC MATTERS

DAY 6

We have been talking about how a relationship with Jesus should affect every part of your life, including the music you listen to. Today I want to give you some alternatives.

You know, some people think Christianity is the religion that says not to do this and not to do that. They think it says that God doesn't want you to have any fun, that He rips you off and that anything fun is sin.

Well, that isn't true. The problem is that the world's idea of fun is mostly sin.

GOD'S IDEA OF FUN IS RIGHTEOUS, RADICAL AND WORLD-CHANGING.

There are a number of incredible Christian groups that play just about any type of music: rap, rock, folk, blues — you name it. You can glorify God in the style of music you really like to listen to.

I want to encourage you to go to your local Christian bookstore and take a look at some of the groups, such as Petra, Carman, Kenny Marks, Rachel Rachel, Whitecross, ETW or White Heart. Every Christian bookstore I've been to has a place where you can listen to the tapes.

Go in and listen to a bunch of tapes before you buy them. If you like what you hear, just go ahead and buy them. But I want to caution you: Don't be addicted to Christian music the way you were addicted to secular music.

The world does not revolve around music; it revolves around Jesus.

People often keep their minds blasted with music because they're afraid to deal with some of the issues in their lives – their hurts, troubles or frustrations. All day long they keep their minds occupied with music, music, music.

When I realized I was doing that, I pulled the radio and the tape player out of my car. I didn't want to be tempted to listen to music all the time. I wanted to have more time to think and pray.

Make a decision now to put righteous, godly music in your heart, in your mind and in your life so you can be transformed.

Do you still remember the verses you learned in the beginning? If not, take five minutes to learn them again today!

Week 5

WHY MUSIC MATTERS

DAY 7

How can you tell if a band is really Christian or not?

There are a lot of groups today that claim to be Christian bands. But when they cross over into secular music, they don't talk about Jesus in their concerts.

How can you tell if a group is really of God?

Let me give you a couple of hints.

First, look at the lifestyles of the group members.

Look at some magazines and read interviews about them. Find out what they're talking about and what they're thinking about. Think about what's going on inside of them. Ask yourself if their goal is really to lift up Jesus or just to be expressive and creative with music.

It is really important to do this.

Some people are barely saved before they start banging out music just as they did before they were saved. They aren't solid; they aren't mature; they're just a bunch of excited Christians. That's great. But you don't want to follow them so closely that if they fall away it messes up your walk with God.

People are just human. We cannot idolize them the way people of the world idolize rock or pop stars. Pop stars come and go, but Jesus doesn't. He stays the same forever.

Another way you can tell if a band is really Christian is to read their lyrics.

 ASK YOURSELF:

What do the lyrics talk about?

How are they trying to influence me?

What ideas are they trying to communicate to me?

Is that something I really want in my head?

Even if the message isn't negative – even if it's neutral – it's occupying your "brain space," and it's not helping you grow closer to God. Is that what you want?

Well, this ends our week of talking about music.

If you haven't done it by now, I want you to have a party.

Go into your room and get all of your tapes and anything else that isn't 100 percent glorifying to God.

Take those tapes, posters and any other musical paraphernalia you have and destroy them.

Unravel those tapes! Snap those CDs! Jump on them! Stomp on them!

Give thanks to God for setting you free from this garbage in your mind and in your life.

Thank Him for putting godly things there. Yes, it is radical and wild, but that is what being a Christian is all about!

NO ONE DESERVES TO STAND IN THE WINNER'S CIRCLE UNLESS HE IS WILLING TO PAY THE PRICE.

Week 6

WHAT IS REAL WORSHIP?

WEEK 6 MEMORY VERSES

JOHN 4:23-24

Yet a time is coming and has now come when the true worshipers will worship the Father in spirit and truth, for they are the kind of worshipers the Father seeks. God is spirit, and His worshipers must worship in spirit and in truth.

PSALM 22:3

But thou art holy, O thou that inhabitest the praises of Israel (KJV).

WHAT IS REAL WORSHIP?

DAY 1

When I was a kid growing up in church, I remember hearing the church leader say, "Now it is time for our call to worship."

I figured it was about time to break out the No Doz because that was when I got bored in church.

WHY ARE SO MANY TEENAGERS BORED BY WORSHIP?

I see teenagers in churches all across America hanging out in the back of the church, crossing their arms and falling asleep, while all the adults are worshipping God. We're letting them have all the fun.

What is real worship? The word itself means "to adore." The literal translation indicates an act of bowing down to kiss the ring of a king or a leader.

When we talk about worshipping God, we are not just talking about singing a few boring old songs. Worship is adoring Him, whether you're a guy or a girl.

You are *not* too cool to bow down and kiss the ring on the hand of the Son of God, who gave His life for you.

Worship is an expression of your love for God. It's similar to having a boyfriend or girlfriend whom you think about all the time. When you get together with that person, you talk about all the neat things you like about him or her. You are showing your adoration. In a sense, you are worshipping that person.

How much more should we worship the King of kings who shed His blood so that we could go to heaven forever? He bought us back from the devil. We don't belong to the devil anymore, and we're not dominated by sin anymore.

Think about real worship as you go to church and as you have your quiet time this week. Worship God and tell Him the awesome things you like about Him.

Write a list of things that you adore now or have adored in the past. Include names of people if you need to.

1.

2.

3.

Write down some things that you said to or about a person that expressed your adoration.

1.

2.

3.

Write a list of things to God that expresses your adoration for Him.

1.

2.

3.

Review the verses you memorized from last week. Meditate on them, and put them in your heart.

Week 6

Day 2

John 4:23-24

> Yet a time is coming and has now come when the true worshipers
> will worship the Father in spirit and truth, for they are the kind of
> worshipers the Father seeks. God is spirit, and his worshipers must
> worship in spirit and in truth.

Read John 4:1-26.

We read earlier that the Bible admonishes us in Ephesians 5 to sing songs,
hymns and spiritual songs, making melody in our hearts to God.

Real worship is not just singing songs that come from a book or from an
overhead projector.

In John 4:1-26, Jesus talks to the Samaritan woman at the well. He says that
true worshippers worship God in Spirit and in truth. Many people are just
singing the words they see projected on a screen. If you are not singing
truthfully from your heart, you are not singing "in truth." It's no wonder you
find worship boring.

Real worship comes from the heart and lifts up Jesus.

Worshipping the Lord in the Spirit is not worshipping Him in the flesh. It is not just getting excited for the sake of getting excited. It is not just getting loud for the sake of getting loud.

It is worshipping Him in your spirit, from your heart. It is closing your eyes and letting your mouth sing what is coming from your heart.

As you sing and worship like this from your heart, it keeps you refreshed. You are letting God know just how cool you think He is.

Your relationship with God will be fresh and alive if you let Him know every day just how incredible you think He is.

I want you to meditate on these verses today from John 4. Meet with your accountability partner, and worship the King of kings together.

IF YOU PAUSE TO THINK, YOU WILL FIND CAUSE TO THANK.

Week 6

WHAT IS REAL WORSHIP?

DAY 3

Read Psalm 119.

We're talking about worship this week.

What does it mean to worship God, and how can we really get into worship? Let me tell you about someone who was really into worship. His name was David, and he wrote most of the worship songs found today in the book of Psalms.

Using the songs that David wrote is a great way to keep your own worship life exciting. I want to turn your attention to the whole book of Psalms, but especially to Psalm 119. In this song David goes on and on and just worships God like crazy.

David says in verse 54, "Your decrees are the theme of my song wherever I lodge." He sang about God's Word wherever he was.

One great way to worship is to take individual psalms and read them as if you wrote them, praising God for how awesome He is.

> Your word is a lamp to my feet and a light for my path (Psalm 119:105).

Oh, how I love your law! I meditate on it all day long. Your commands make me wiser than my enemies, for they are ever with me (Psalm 119:97-98).

David goes on praising God for His Word.

My eyes stay open through the watches of the night, that I may meditate on your promises (Psalm 119:148).

Speaking of his excitement about God, he said,

My zeal wears me out (Psalm 119:139).

Look what he says in verse 164:

Seven times a day I praise you for your righteous laws.

And in verse 171 he says,

May my lips overflow with praise, for you teach me your decrees.

As you take these verses and begin to read them aloud to God, you'll get excited about Him for what He's done. Make them your own words of praise, and have your own worship service with God.

Take seven minutes and read the verses I have listed here. Say them over and over again as if you wrote them to God yourself. Speak them to Him, and have a mini worship service right now. Then take them with you, and keep them on your lips to praise Him with all day long.

COMMIT YOURSELF TO WORSHIP GOD THIS WEEK AS NEVER BEFORE.

Week 6

WHAT IS REAL WORSHIP?

DAY 4

Psalm 22:3

But thou art holy, O thou that inhabitest the praises of Israel (KJV).

Spend a couple of minutes meditating on this verse. What does it mean to you?

It's actually very simple to explain this verse. When God finds people who are really praising Him, who are really worshipping Him, who are genuinely singing from their hearts, then He comes and "inhabits" their praises. In other words, as you praise Him, He is right there with you — He comes and hangs out with you.

Some people think, Man, how do I get into the presence of God? It seems like I pray, but I can't really get in there. I go to church, but it seems like God's presence isn't really there.

Let me tell you what other people in your church are feeling, people who are worshipping God and basking in His presence. They're feeling the awesomeness of God right there with them. You won't experience His presence unless you focus *your* attention on Him and sing from *your* heart to Him.

For you to experience God's presence in your quiet times or in a church service, it is important for you to close your eyes and think about the words you're singing. You have to sing them from your heart and truly worship God.

God guarantees that if you will do that, He will be there – and His awesome presence will blow your mind!

Take five minutes now and think of all the great things He has done for you, and then *thank* Him. List ten of them here:

1.

2.

3.

4.

5.

6.

7.

8.

9.

10.

Now genuinely thank God for all these things. Worship Him using the Scripture verses you learned yesterday.

A THANKFUL PERSON IS A HAPPY PERSON.

Week 6

WHAT IS REAL WORSHIP?

DAY 5

L et's talk about praise for a few minutes today.

Praise and worship are different actions. They both involve words that come from your mouth, but praise is celebration and worship is adoration. It is important for you to have a time of praise and to begin to celebrate how awesome God is and what an exciting thing He has done in your life.

For example, the day Moses crossed the Red Sea with all of Israel, Pharaoh's army drowned trying to follow them across. When that happened, guess what Moses and Israel did? They had a hoedown! They started going crazy. They were totally excited because God had rescued them. You can find this in Exodus 14 and 15. Read that passage now.

God has rescued you from something even greater.

HOW MUCH MORE SHOULD YOU CELEBRATE BECAUSE OF WHAT GOD HAS RESCUED YOU FROM?

Praise is just that.

It's a celebration.

In fact, one definition says praise is going into a "rage" of exhilarating excitement to God, a rage of celebration because of what He has done for you.

I want you to take a minute right where you are. Nobody is looking. I want you to think about the incredible things God has done for you. Just begin to celebrate.

You might think it's weird, but you're going to be celebrating like this for thousands of years in heaven. You might as well get all the practice you can right now.

Memorize the verses from this week, and get them into your heart!

List some of the things you know God has done for you.

1.

2.

3.

4.

Praise and celebrate God now for all that He has done.

Week 6

WHAT IS REAL WORSHIP?

DAY 6

Review Ephesians 5:19-20.

The Bible says we are to make a melody in our hearts to God. What does this really mean?

Well, God is interested in hearing the words from your heart.

Yes, you can sing a song from an overhead projector or from a hymnal and cause those words to come from your heart. But even more intimate is a song that you make up and sing from your heart to God's heart. Today's verse says, "Make music in your heart to the Lord."

MAKE UP YOUR OWN SONG TO GOD.

I remember when I wrote a song to my wife, Katie, while we were dating. It meant so much to her because she knew it came from my heart. The same thing happens when you, from your heart, write a song to God.

Hannah, my three-year-old daughter, and Charity, my two-year-old, often walk around the house singing songs. Sometimes they sing about the Lord. Sometimes they sing about a dog or a cat, and they're just singing little melodies from their hearts. I like to sit and listen to them, even though they're off tune sometimes and don't always make sense. As their father, just listening to them express joy from their hearts gives me great joy.

That's what singing and making music in your heart to God is all about. It's about singing a new song to Him.

Sometimes in a worship service you'll hear a song that begins spontaneously. That's the time for you to worship God and make up your own words. Make up your own melody and sing to Him from a new heart. Sing to Him a new song. In your own words, simply tell Him how much you love Him.

Let it come from your heart. As you do, the presence of God will fall on you, and your experience with Him will escalate to a new level of intensity.

Take a moment right now to worship God with a couple of songs you know. Then make up your own tune and let Jesus know how much you love Him today.

Meet with your accountability partner, and worship God together.

WHAT IS REAL WORSHIP?

DAY 7

God wants us to be people who can praise Him when we're alone or in a crowd. I want to encourage you today to make a decision to be a worshipper.

Make a decision – praise God no matter what circumstances you are in. Praise God when times are tough, and praise God because He is going to get you through them.

Praise God because He has given you favor.

Praise God whether you are alone or with other people.

Praise God when you're in your youth group and no one else is praising Him.

Praise God with your accountability partner. Really worship God together. Do not be someone who only celebrates when he feels peer pressure to celebrate.

You make the decision – the same way you made a decision to have quiet time. Demand that your lips praise God; demand that your mind be focused; demand that your heart sing to God.

Whether you feel like it or not, God is worthy because:

He is awesome.

He is incredible.

He created the world.

He spoke, and everything came into existence.

He will be around forever.

He is God.

He is the only One who is worthy of our adoration. He is the only One who is worthy of our hearts. He is the only One who is worthy of our praise and our music.

Make a decision today to be a worshipper. Worship God every day in your quiet time, and worship Him every chance you get during a worship service.

Be someone who lets words of praise and worship come from your lips, no matter what circumstances you face.

Take five minutes and worship God using all that you have learned this week!

Review the verses you memorized this week. Chew on them until your heart is nourished!

Week 7

Friends for Life

Week 7 Memory Verses

JOHN 15:15
I no longer call you servants, because a servant does not know his master's business. Instead, I have called you friends, for everything that I learned from my father I have made known to you.

PROVERBS 13:20
He who walks with the wise grows wise, but a companion of fools suffers harm.

PROVERBS 27:6
Wounds from a friend can be trusted, but an enemy multiplies kisses.

JOHN 15:13
Greater love has no one than this, that he lay down his life for his friends.

PROVERBS 18:24
A friend must show himself friendly.

Week 7

FRIENDS FOR LIFE

DAY 1

If you have had an awesome, mind-blowing, life-changing, heart-to-heart, face-to-face encounter with the living God, it will affect *every* area of your life.

That includes your friendships.

Let's talk about the world's definition of a friendship and what the world looks for in a friend.

Most of the time when you see people who are friends in the world, it's because they found themselves in the same social setting. They like the same music. They like to do drugs together. They like the same kinds of movies. They dress the same, play the same sports or have the same activities.

So they call each other friends. But often these people who call each other friends are really just out to take advantage of each other.

They do not know each other's goals or dreams or fears. They do not know each other's priorities. They do not really know the direction each other's lives are taking. They do not know anything about each other. They are really just associates who hang out together.

REAL FRIENDS CARE ABOUT WHAT IS GOING ON IN EACH OTHER'S LIVES.

Many times a person hesitates to become a Christian because of what his friends will say. In reality, these "friends" are mere acquaintances in the same social framework. That person's friends would not do anything for him. They wouldn't stand up for him or stick with him. Yet when that person becomes a Christian, he is so afraid of what his "friends" will think.

I want you to think for a minute if there were people in your life who were acquaintances but not really friends. Think of people you ran around with – either before you were a Christian or after you became a Christian. Include people you never got to know because you only ran around together.

List some people you would call "friends" now but know very little about.

1.

2.

3.

List some people you are really getting to know or would like to become *real* friends with.

1.

2.

3.

Pray this prayer today:

"Jesus, teach me what it means to be a real friend, and give me the opportunity to make some deep, Christian friendships this month. In Your name, amen."

WE SERVE OTHERS BEST WHEN WE LOVE FIRST.

Week 7

FRIENDS FOR LIFE

DAY 2

John 15:15

> I no longer call you servants, because a servant does not know his master's business. Instead, I have called you friends, for everything that I learned from my Father I have made known to you.

Today we are going to look at what the Bible says *real* friends are. We find Jesus' definition of friendship in John 15:15. Jesus was saying:

> Up until this time you guys have been serving Me, following Me, hanging out with Me as acquaintances and servants. But from now on I am going to call you My friends because I have shared everything with you that My Father has shared with Me.

> I have wanted to tell everybody, but I did not. I just shared My heart with you guys. You know what is going on in My heart. You know what is going on in My mind. You really know Me. You are My friends.

Real friendship is sharing your heart. It is being real. It is sharing part of yourself with somebody else.

We must learn to be truly honest, especially when it comes to girls and guys. We either date them or hate them. We don't know how to make friends with the opposite sex or share our hearts. We're afraid they might not like us.

Let's work on developing some godly friendships based on the principles Jesus used.

Jesus says, "You guys are qualified to be My friends because I have shared My heart with you."

Think of some people with whom you could share your heart and really be yourself: your parents? someone at church? someone at your youth group? a relative? Write down their names.

1.

2.

3.

Write down a few things you want to share with them.

Make a special appointment to do it. Tell them you want to share some things with them.

As you develop some awesome, godly friendships, these friends will help you to stand in the Lord when things get tough.

WITHOUT ACCOUNTABILITY, THERE IS NO MOTIVATION FOR CHANGE.

Week 7

FRIENDS FOR LIFE

DAY 3

Proverbs 13:20

> He who walks with the wise grows wise, but a companion of fools suffers harm.

Spend some time meditating on this verse. What does it mean to you?

It is very important how you choose your friends, now that you have decided to live for God 100 percent.

You can't just hang around a bunch of halfhearted Christians who do not really give a rip about God, or people who are lukewarm for God. Why? Because a companion of fools will suffer harm. If you hang around fools, you're going to suffer harm.

The Bible says in Psalm 14:1: "The fool says in his heart, 'There is no God.'"

If you hang around people who are not Christians, you are hanging around fools. They are saying that God is not there. You're suffering harm because they will influence you to turn away from God.

Just believe the Word of God. Don't wait for it to be proved to you. If you hang around those people, harm will come to you.

If you want to be incredibly smart or have supernatural insight, you have to hang around people who are that way.

You have to hang around people who are tight with God.

List some people you have hung out with recently who are not wise. They're really not following God; they're just more of an acquaintance to you.

1.

2.

3.

Now seriously consider how much time you spend with them.

Katie and I came to a point in our lives a couple of years ago when we had to decide who we were going to spend time with. We had so many friends, former friends and people we'd known for a long time, who always wanted to come over and spend time with us. These people were just acquaintances, people to whom we really had to minister. They did not lift us up.

Don't get me wrong — it is important to minister to people. In a friendship, however, each person must be able to encourage and to learn from the other. If this mutual exchange doesn't occur regularly, it is not a friendship but a ministry. Are your friends always dragging you down, or are they pulling you up?

We had to make some tough decisions about whom we would spend time with — even about whom we would give our phone number to.

I challenge you to make some of those tough decisions today. Think about whom you really spend your time with.

Are they real friends or just acquaintances?

DECIDE TO SPEND YOUR TIME WITH PEOPLE WHO ARE WISE IN THE LORD SO THAT YOU MAY GROW WISER.

FRIENDS FOR LIFE

DAY 4

Proverbs 27:6

Wounds from a friend can be trusted, but an enemy multiplies kisses.

Spend three minutes meditating on this verse. What does it mean to you?

Many times friends in the world will only tell you things that you want to hear. They say things like: You look great. You look pretty. You are so cool.

A real friend goes deeper than that. He is somebody who is wise, somebody you can share your heart with, somebody who is not afraid to tell you something that could hurt your feelings but would help you in the long run.

A real friend does not let a friend walk around with mustard on his face. He tells him to wipe it off. A real friend will not let you run around with mascara running down your face. She tells you to wipe it off.

If you are going to be a real friend, you have to be willing to let people speak into your life. Maybe they will say things like: Hey, I see you have been getting angry a lot. That's not really like Jesus. Or, I see that you are really selfish. I see that you have a bad attitude. I see that you are not very submissive to your parents.

Let them speak into your life.

It is not that you are passing judgment on each other; you are helping each other grow. Sometimes friends can see things in your life that you can't see.

The wounds of a friend can be trusted. It might hurt a little, or it might wound you when a friend tells you the truth, but that person can be trusted. You want those kinds of wounds.

You do not want wounds from friends who are just cutting you down for the sake of cutting you down. That's what happens in the world.

They stab each other in the back. They chew each other up and spit each other out just to make themselves look cool.

The wounds of a true friend can be trusted because they are going to help you examine your life and become more godly.

Think of some people in your life from whom you could receive honest input. Write down a few names.

1.

2.

3.

Go to these people – maybe it's your accountability partner or your parents – and ask them to help you grow stronger in the Lord.

If they see something in your life that does not match up to the Bible, then ask them to speak that honestly to you.

Tell them that you are not going to be offended or hurt but that you are going to pray about these things. This is pretty heavy-duty, but this is what *real* friendship is all about.

Review the verses from this past week. Get them into your heart.

FRIENDS FOR LIFE

DAY 5

 ohn 15:13

> Greater love has no one than this, that he lay down his life for his friends.

Take some time out today to get this verse into your heart.

Jesus laid down His life for us. He was a true friend to us even when we did not deserve such a true friend.

You know that laying down your life does not just mean dying on a cross.

It also means laying down your selfishness, laying down your priorities, laying down your agenda to help somebody else.

A real friend will lay down his time even when he's really, really busy.

Slam on the breaks of life.

Stop.

Listen.

Care.

Laying down your life means rearranging your priorities so you can be sensitive to other people. You can be a friend to them even though they are not a friend to you. You can minister to them.

You must be willing to lay down your busy life and the things you think are important to you. Why? Because there is something more important: a person who needs someone to listen. Write out John 15:13 in your own words.

Write out some things you can do today that would be a dramatic symbol of laying down part of your life to be a friend to someone else.

Share with your accountability partner the new commitments you've made this week.

FRIENDS FOR LIFE

DAY 6

We have been talking about friendships this week – about how to make awesome, incredible, radical friendships.

It is important to teenagers to be in a network of people they like, people they think are cool, people they can hang with, people they get along with. You find your identity with the group of people you hang out with.

When you ask some teenagers what they do, they say, "I'm in band," or "I'm in sports." The group of friends you surround yourself with can affect your life in a powerful way.

 **DO YOU WANT TO BE LIKE YOUR FRIENDS?**

When you become a Christian, the natural thing to do is to go and tell all your friends about Jesus. You want to keep your friends and just add going to church to your life. There will be a point, however, when you will have to make a decision about what kind of people you are going to surround yourself with. You have to decide if you are going to straddle the fence and try to have some Christian friends and some worldly friends.

However, those worldly friends will continue to influence you. You cannot be with cussing, drinking and partying people without their influence working its way into your life, ultimately dragging you away from God.

It is very important that you surround yourself with radical Christian friends. Get into a radically turned-on youth group.

CHANGE THE WORLD – START WITH ONE PERSON.

Start with at least one other radical friend, and then find others. These are the people you should hang around with and share your heart with.

Some people have their "real friends" at school, who are heathens, and their Christian friends at church, who they don't even hang around with.

Our Christian friends are the people we need to hang with because these are the people who really love God.

It is a matter of being honest and laying out the guidelines you want to have for friendships. Look at Jesus' friendships with His disciples. These were the people He hung with.

He ministered to prostitutes and other people, but the people He hung out with were the people He could trust and listen to. They were people who would listen to Him, who would listen to His heart. This is spiritual survival!

Make a list of some acquaintances who have *not* affected your life positively.

1.

2.

3.

Pray that God would really intervene in their lives.

Decide that if there is not a change in these relationships within a certain period of time, you will walk away from them. Until God changes their hearts, the only reason you're going to communicate with them is to try to win them to the Lord.

Week 7

FRIENDS FOR LIFE

DAY 7

Proverbs 18:24

A man who has friends must himself be friendly (NKJV).

Write this verse out in your own words.

This verse means that you can't wait for people to come to you and say, "Please be my godly friend."

Some people complain:

> I do not have any friends.

> I do not have anybody to share my heart with.

> I do not have people who run to my door asking me to do things or calling me all the time.

You have to be the one to show yourself friendly. You have to be the one who takes the first step to say that you want to be a godly friend. Be somebody who shares his heart, somebody who is honest with people, somebody who will lay down his life. You be that person, the one to initiate that kind of friendship.

You might think that would be too hard because you are shy.

But 2 Timothy 1:7 tells you, "For God did not give us a spirit of timidity, but of power, of love and of self-discipline."

He has given you power, love and self-discipline. He has not given you timidity. Shyness is not from God.

You need to take the initiative to show yourself friendly. Target some people and pray for godly, awesome friendships. Pull them aside and tell them you want to develop some incredibly wild, godly friendships.

Find people you can share your heart with, who do not talk about others behind their backs, who encourage others and help them grow in the Lord.

Then ask them to be that kind of friend with you. Ask them if they would be willing to keep pushing you toward God and if you can help push them into a closer relationship with God.

A friend must show himself friendly. You have to be the initiator, the one to step out of your comfort zone today.

Pray about the people we talked about this week and the people you listed. Find out who can be your real friends, and take the time this week to approach them and establish the kinds of parameters you want to have. Establish the kind of godly friendships you want and invite your real friends to be a part.

You are destined to be a successful Christian if you surround yourself with these kinds of friends. They will not let you fall, and you will not let them fall.

COURAGE IS DECIDING YOU WILL NOT BE INFLUENCED BY FEAR.

> Talk with your friends about going on a missions trip this year.
> It would be a life-changing experience for all of you.

Week 8

HOW TO PRAY

Week 8 Memory Verses

MATTHEW 6:9-13
Our Father in heaven, hallowed be your name, your kingdom come, your will be done on earth as it is in heaven. Give us today our daily bread. Forgive us our debts, as we also have forgiven our debtors. And lead us not into temptation, but deliver us from the evil one.

MATTHEW 7:7
Ask and it will be given to you; seek and you will find; knock and the door will be opened to you.

MATTHEW 6:7-8
And when you pray, do not keep on babbling like pagans, for they think they will be heard because of their many words. Do not be like them, for your Father knows what you need before you ask him.

1 JOHN 5:14-15
This is the confidence we have in approaching God: that if we ask anything according to His will, he hears us. And if we know that he hears us — whatever we ask — we know that we have what we asked of him.

Week 8

How to Pray

Day 1

Matthew 6:9-13

> Our Father in heaven, hallowed be your name, your kingdom come, your will be done on earth as it is in heaven. Give us today our daily bread. Forgive us our debts, as we also have forgiven our debtors. And lead us not into temptation, but deliver us from the evil one.

Take a few minutes to memorize these verses. Write them again in your own words.

Many of us take for granted that we know how to pray. When you get saved, you are told to read your Bible, go to church and pray.

 **What does it really mean to pray?**

First of all, prayer is communication; it is communing with God. It is your heart and His heart joining together. You are listening to Him, and He is listening to you. Jesus set the example for prayer in Matthew 6:9-13.

He began prayer by saying, "Our Father in heaven, hallowed be your name."

He wants us to start with praise and worship, going into His gates with thanksgiving and entering His courts with praise. This is really worshipping Him. Spend the first few minutes of your prayer time worshipping God and getting into His presence.

In verse 10 He says, "Your kingdom come, your will be done."

Whatever we ask, we ask for His will, way and heart to come through it.

1. Ask for His kingdom to come in your life. Ask that every part of your life would line up with His words and that every part of your heart would be overcome by His kingdom.

2. Ask that His will would be done in your family.

3. Pray that His will would be done in your school, in your youth group, in your church.

4. Most of all, pray for His will to be done and His kingdom to come in this world. God is looking for people who will agree with Him and ask Him to do what He really wants to do.

Jesus then goes on to say, "Give us today our daily bread."

Ask God to provide your needs today. When you pray and ask Him to meet your needs, you are not praying selfishly. Begin to praise Him and say, "Lord, I know You are so awesome that You supply all my needs. I know You can do this."

Be sure that you have forgiveness in your heart, or He is not going to hear your prayer. In verse 12 Jesus says, "Forgive us our debts, as we also have forgiven our debtors." Don't be mad at other people and hold unforgiveness in your heart.

End your prayer with praise and worship in His presence.

This is simply an outline that you can expand on to have an incredibly *wild* prayer life.

This week we are going to talk about different aspects of prayer to help you understand how to have awesome times with Jesus every time you pray.

Take seven minutes and pray right now using the outline that Jesus gave us.

Week 8

HOW TO PRAY

DAY 2

Matthew 7:7

Ask and it will be given to you; seek and you will find; knock and the door will be opened to you.

Take two minutes now and memorize this verse.

Many times we do not receive things because we do not ask for them, or we ask with a wrong motive in our hearts (see James 4:2-3).

Jesus simply wants us to ask for the things we need. He guarantees that if we ask according to His will, then we will receive it as long as we pray with a right motive.

Many times we have selfish or prideful motives, or we want something that will make us look good rather than glorify Him. The proper motive is that He would be glorified and that His gospel would be made known. Whatever you ask for should be for His glory, not for your selfishness.

For example, many times when we ask for people to get saved, we are asking because we want them to go to heaven. Unfortunately, that is a selfish motive. You may even be praying for your mom or dad to be saved. But God will not answer that prayer just because you love them.

 **WHY DOES GOD ANSWER PRAYER?**

He will answer prayer because it is His desire for His kingdom to come and His will to be done.

Ask with a proper motive. Say, "God, I want my mom and dad to be saved because You love them, and You want them to go to heaven. You care about them, and it is just because You care that I want them to be saved and to go to heaven. Jesus, You shed Your blood for them, and You love them much more than I do. Please save them — and glorify Yourself!"

Make a list of some things you can unselfishly ask the Lord for that will glorify Him.

1.

2.

3.

4.

Meditate on the Lord's prayer all day!

Week 8

HOW TO PRAY

DAY 3

Matthew 6:7-8

And when you pray, do not keep on babbling like pagans, for they think they will be heard because of their many words. Do not be like them, for your Father knows what you need before you ask him.

Take five minutes today and memorize these verses.

Do not let your prayers become ritualistic.

Many times we get into a ritual of praying the same words over and over. (Now I lay me down to sleep....) They become lifeless and meaningless prayers.

We start to pray like the Hindus or Muslims. They pray the same words and just chant them over and over. They think they are going to be heard for praying so many words.

Jesus said not to repeat your words over and over. It is not wrong to repeat, but it is wrong to repeat words without meaning.

Our prayer life is not just a ritual.

It is an encounter with the living God.

It is Him hearing us and us hearing Him.

It is a chance to have heart-to-heart, face-to-face contact with God.

Even if you ask for the same things several different times, make sure you are having a fresh encounter with God. Make sure you are worshipping Him and asking Him for those things because they will glorify Him.

Make it an encounter with God, not just a time to ask for a lot of things. Some people go into prayer with a list, instead of sensing God's heart and then asking Him to do what He wants to do in the situation.

Our prayer time can become a habit of repeating requests for things we really want. We can even begin to act like we are begging Him for what we want. We do not need to beg; we just need to remind Him that it is something He wants to do and thank Him for sending the answer.

Do not let prayer become a ritual of requesting. Let it be an encounter with God every time!

Week 8

HOW TO PRAY

DAY 4

1 John 5:14-15

> This is the confidence we have in approaching God: that if we ask anything according to His will, he hears us. And if we know that he hears us — whatever we ask — we know that we have what we asked of him.

Take five minutes to memorize this verse now.

As we pray "Your kingdom come, Your will be done," it's very important to find out what God's will is and then pray for it to be done.

It is important to remind God of His Word.

To do that, you have to know His Word. That is why we have been talking about renewing your mind with the Word of God and memorizing Scripture all the time. The more Scripture you know, the more prayers you are going to have answered.

When you pray, you can pray according to His will and His Word, and with confidence.

You can say, "God, it is Your desire to do this because Your Word says so right here."

For example, you can say:

> Lord, I know that you want to meet all my needs because the Bible says in Philippians 4:19, "My God will meet all your needs according to his glorious riches in Christ Jesus." So, Lord, in Jesus' name, I have confidence that You will fulfill this need in my life.

Use Scripture to back up your requests.

Look at the verses you memorized. They say that if you want God to hear you, you have to ask according to His will. How do you know if you are asking according to His will? When you ask according to His Word.

If you want effective prayers that change you and change the world, then you have to remind God of His Word.

He is not moved to act by your tears.

He is not moved by your whining.

He is moved by His Word.

Pray that laborers would take the gospel to the unreached people groups of the world! Pray about being one of those laborers. Get information about taking a missions trip (there's some in the back of this book) and really ask the Lord if it's for you to do.

Week 8

DAY 5

How can you keep your prayers full of life?

Many people believe their prayer lives are dry and dull. It seems like they just can't break through. They say they pray, but it just does not seem like God is there.

If you are having a hard time breaking through to God, let me give you a hint that will help you to keep your prayer times fresh every day.

 ASK YOURSELF THESE QUESTIONS:

What sin do I have in my life that is keeping me from breaking through?

What area of my life am I hanging on to and not letting God deal with?

Am I preventing Jesus from being Lord of something in my life?

What is keeping me from having the full encounter with God that I can have?

Now, just sit and listen for a few minutes. God will open your eyes. He'll begin to speak to you.

We need to keep examining our lives and letting Him purify our hearts. If we stop, our hearts begin to harden, and we can't hear Him anymore.

One essential ingredient to an awesome prayer life is constantly asking God what else He desires to refine and take out of you. It should not be the same thing every time.

You should be getting more and more godly and more and more holy. The junk should be coming out of your life.

So ask Him: "Lord, what should I be getting out of my life?" or "Lord, what needs to be purified?"

Maybe it's jealousy.

Maybe it's pride or the way you treat people.

Maybe it's your attitude.

Ask Him to purify your heart. Psalm 51:10 says: "Create in me a pure heart, O God, and renew a steadfast spirit within me."

Take three minutes and meditate on this verse.

If we come to God with that kind of attitude, we can be sure that we will have a fresh encounter with Him every day.

Ask Him today what He wants to clean out of your life. Have a great time of prayer!

Review the verses that you have memorized this week.

Week 8

How to Pray

Day 6

It is important to remember not to be selfish in your prayer life.

Most people only pray about things that affect their own lives.

People are only concerned with how they can be blessed, how their families can be blessed, how their school can be blessed.

It's so easy to think, me, me, me! That's the kind of society we live in today. Everyone is concerned with me, myself and I.

A HEALTHY SIGN OF AN INCREDIBLE PRAYER LIFE IS WHEN YOU PRAY FOR THINGS THAT DON'T NECESSARILY BENEFIT YOU.

Pray for the world and for specific countries.

Pray for leaders around the world.

Pray for church leaders.

Pray for your friends.

Pray for your future and for the futures of your friends.

Pray for people you are going to witness to.

The Bible admonishes us to pray for our leaders and to lift them up and to pour out our hearts in prayer for them (see 1 Timothy 2:1-2).

Philippians 4:6 says, "Do not be anxious about anything, but in everything, by prayer and petition, with thanksgiving, present your requests to God."

If you can keep yourself from being selfish in your prayers, then your life will be full because your prayer time is affecting the world around you.

Make a list of some things you can pray for that are unselfish and have nothing to do with blessing your life.

1.

2.

3.

4.

Are you making a difference in the world? Start today by praying for the people of the world!

HOW TO PRAY

DAY 7

I want to turn your attention to one of Jesus' most incredible moments in prayer. It is the time when He was on the Mount of Transfiguration.

Read the story in Luke 9:28-35.

Notice the Bible does not say Jesus went up onto a mountain to be transfigured. It says that He took His disciples up *to pray*.

They were praying, and suddenly Elijah and Moses showed up. They started hanging out and talking together, and suddenly the presence of God came. His presence was so incredible that God began to speak audibly – and Jesus began to glow!

Jesus was just going to the mountain to hang out with His Father and pray as He always did. There is no indication in the scriptural account that this prayer time was going to be different from any of His other prayer times.

Just imagine the kind of quiet times you could have with God, just hanging out with Him, getting intimate, hearing His voice and hearing His heart.

GET INTO THE AWESOME PRESENCE OF THE LIVING GOD. JESUS ENCOUNTERED THE GLORY OF GOD THROUGH PRAYER. SO CAN YOU.

Think about the commitment of keeping your prayer time sacred and holy before God.

To pray every day and to meet God in your prayer closet is more important than meeting with the president of the United States.

Allow God to transfigure your mind, your heart and your face so that you become more like Him every day and continually bring His light to the world.

You can become a world-changer every day just because you have met with Him in secret and have received His power in your life for the day.

You've finished *Fifty-Six Days Ablaze* — good job!

You've been learning and growing in the Lord like never before, so don't let it stop with the end of this book.

Keep on meeting regularly with your accountability partner. Keep pushing each other to grow deeper and deeper in the Lord.

Review your memory verses until they are a permanent part of you. It's the Word that will keep you strong.

Stay close to God in prayer. Prayer is real communication with God. It's not just a ritual. It makes a difference when you do it.

Keep reading good books and going to meetings that will challenge you to grow in the Lord. If you're interested in the next devotional from Ron Luce, contact Teen Mania Ministries.

Finally, think and pray about going on a missions trip. A missions trip is an awesome opportunity for God to use you and show you more about Himself.

IF YOU SEEK GOD WITH ALL YOUR HEART, HE WILL REVEAL HIS WILL TO YOU.

MISSIONS TRIPS

Teen Mania puts together missions trips during summers and Christmas breaks so that teenagers like you can put their faith into action.

"Teen Maniacs" have reached over three hundred thousand people for Jesus Christ since Teen Mania started in 1986.

God will use you to change people's lives while you are on a missions trip. But He will also change you beyond your wildest imagination.

ACQUIRE THE FIRE CONVENTIONS

Acquire the Fire Youth Conventions are action-packed, two-day events where you (along with thousands of other teenagers) can gather together to encounter God.

Ron Luce uses contemporary praise and worship, hilarious skits, high-tech equipment and multiscreen video to tell you what it means to serve a powerful, living God.

Conventions are held in more than twenty major cities throughout the United States and Canada, including Miami, Denver, Los Angeles and Edmonton.

Find out how you can be a part of the missions trips, internship program or Acquire the Fire conventions. Contact us today at:

Teen Mania Ministries
P.O. Box 700721
Tulsa, OK 74170-0721
Phone: (918) 496-1891
or 1-800-299-TEEN

I Made a Decision

. . . .

If you've made a commitment to Jesus Christ, please fill out this form. Give it to a pastor or leader if you're at a Teen Mania meeting or mail it to Teen Mania Ministries, P.O. Box 700721, Tulsa, OK 74170-0721.

Your Name _____

Address _____

City _____ State _____ Zip _____

Phone _____

Do you currently attend a church? ☐ Yes ☐ No

Name of church _____

☐ I am giving my life to Jesus for the first time.

_____
Date

☐ I am recommitting my life to Jesus.

☐ Please send information to help me grow in the Lord.

Name of friend you came with (if applicable)

_____